Skyways

CW01652479

ENTERTAINMENT PLAY

Betty Root

The Theatre Play

	Cast
Cleaning ladies:	**Sally** **Madge** **Queenie**
Caretakers:	**Alf** **Harry**
Superviser:	**Mr Franks**

(Inside the theatre, near the stage.)

Sally: Hello, Madge.

(Madge takes off her coat and puts on an overall.)

Madge: Hello, Sally. Brrr . . . it's cold outside.

Sally: Have a cup of tea.

Madge: Mmmm . . . Thanks, that's better.

Sally: Did I tell you? We've got a new girl starting today.

Madge: No, Sally, how did you manage that?

Sally: I told him.

Madge: Who, Sally?

Sally: Mr Franks. I told him we can't keep the place clean without someone to help us.

Madge: What did he say?

Sally: He didn't like it.

Madge: No, he wouldn't.

Sally: So, we've got a girl starting today.

Madge: Well done, Sally.

Sally: I told him we couldn't manage without some help. Another cup of tea, Madge?

(Later that morning. Madge and Sally are cleaning the stage. Enter Alf and Queenie.)

Alf: Hello, girls, look who's here. This is Queenie, she's come to help you.

Madge: Hello, Queenie, pleased you could come.

Sally: Hello, Queenie, I hope you'll enjoy working here.

Queenie: I know I will.

Sally: Have you worked in a theatre?

Queenie: No, but I've always wanted to. What's on here at the moment?

Madge: Puss-in-Boots.

Queenie: What's it like working here?

Madge: Lovely, isn't it Alf?

Alf: Well, it's all right if you can put up with Madge and Sally.

Sally: Hear that, Madge? I've a good mind to hit you one.

(Sally pretends to hit him with her broom).

(In the theatre just before the afternoon performance.)

Queenie: Can we stay and watch?

Madge: Yes, but keep out of the way.

Sally: And mind the scenery.

Alf: And don't make a noise.

Queenie: Who is that over there?

Madge: That's Pearl, she's the star of the show.

Queenie: I'd like to be the star of the show.

Madge: Shut your eyes and wish.

Queenie: No.

Madge: Why not?

Queenie: No, I can't do that.

Madge: Go on.

Queenie: I don't think wishes come true.

(Enter Alf.)

Alf: What's she telling you now, Queenie?

Queenie: She wants me to shut my eyes and wish.

Madge: But she won't.

Alf: Why not try it?

Madge: There you are, go on, have a go.

(Queenie shuts her eyes.)

Queenie: I wish . . . I wish . . . I wish I was a star and could be the leading lady and . . .

Alf: You'd better open your eyes, the show is about to go on.

(A week later. Alf is talking to Harry.)

Alf: I see Queenie is in her usual place.

Harry: She hasn't missed a show all week.

Alf: She listens carefully to everything they say.

Harry: She must know it all by now.

Alf: Of course she doesn't know it all.

Harry: I expect she does. She's seen it lots of times.

Alf: She couldn't get to know it all in just a week.

Harry: How do you know?

(Alf and Harry go across to Queenie.)

Harry: Are you going to watch it again?

Queenie: Just once more. I know everything that happens.

Harry: Do you know everything they say?

Queenie: Yes, I know it all.

Harry: There you are, I told you so.

Alf: Yes, yes all right.

Queenie: I could do the dancing too.

Alf: I expect you would like to be the star yourself?

Harry: Of course she would, I'd be surprised if she didn't.

Alf: Perhaps she wouldn't want to. Perhaps she'd rather watch.

(Alf and Harry go off arguing.)

Queenie: I wish I could be the star of the show, that would be wonderful.

(Next morning Madge and Sally arrive at the theatre together.)

Sally: What a morning. Brr . . . I'm cold.

Madge: Quick! Put the kettle on and we'll have a hot cup of coffee.

Sally: That's better.

Madge: Queenie's late.

Sally: Here she comes now.

Madge: Hello, Queenie, what's it like outside?

Queenie: It's getting very cold and its snowing hard.

Madge: Are you feeling all right?

Queenie: I'm all right, I'm just very cold.

Sally: Here we are, this will make you feel better.

(Sally gives her a cup of coffee.)

Alf: Have you got a cup for me?

Sally: Help yourself.

(Enter Mr Franks.)

Mr Franks: Come on everyone, there's lots of work to do.

Alf: Yes, Mr Franks, we're just having a quick cup of coffee.

Sally: To warm us up.

Mr Franks: It is very cold I must say. But don't be too long. Will you move some scenery, when you've finished?

(Mr Franks hurries off.)

Alf: It's all right for him, he can have a cup of tea when he likes.

Harry: I've just looked outside and it's snowing very hard.

Queenie: Perhaps Pearl won't be able to get here.

Sally: And they'll ask you to take her place.

Madge: And you'll be a great success.

Harry: And everyone will cheer you.

Alf: That won't happen, they wouldn't ask Queenie.

Harry: They might.

Alf: No they won't.

Harry: If I tell them she knows everything they say.

Alf: No they wouldn't.

Harry: And I tell them she can dance, then they would.

Madge: I expect Pearl will arrive as usual.

Queenie: Yes, I expect she will.

(Later in the day.)

Sally: It hasn't stopped snowing all day.

Madge: I know.

(Enter Mr Franks.)

Mr Franks: You can all go home early girls, in case you can't get home later.

Madge: Thank you, Mr Franks. Will the show go on as usual?

Mr Franks: Oh yes. Some people have arrived early.

Sally: Is everything all right then?

Mr Franks: I'm worried because Pearl hasn't arrived yet.

Queenie: I think I'll stay a little longer.

Sally: If Pearl doesn't turn up, Queenie could take her place.

Queenie: I know all of the show.

Mr Franks: Well, perhaps I will call on you to help.

(Telephone rings and Mr Franks runs to answer it.)

Sally: Do you think that's Pearl to say she can't come?

Madge: It could be.

Sally: I think your wish is coming true.

Madge: I told you.

Queenie: I do wish it would.

Sally: I can't go now.

Madge: Neither can I.

Sally: We will wait and see what happens.

(Enter Alf and Harry.)

Alf: Aren't you going home girls?

Harry: It's still snowing outside.

Alf: Go home while you can.

Harry: I'd stay here if I were you.

Alf: They can't stay here.

Harry: Yes they can.

Sally: We don't mind staying.

Harry: Better to stay here than go home in the snow.

Alf: Why do you always argue with me, Harry?

Harry: I don't, it's you who argues with me.

(Alf and Harry go off arguing.)

Sally: I'm not going home.

Madge: Neither am I.

(Mr Franks shouts from his office.)

Mr Franks: Queenie! Will you come here, please.

Queenie: Yes, Mr Franks.

Sally: Quickly, Queenie! He's going to ask you to play Dick Whittington.

(Queenie rushes off.)

Madge: Let's find a good place to watch.

Sally:	We can see everything from here.
Madge:	There aren't many people here.
Sally:	I expect most have stayed at home.
Madge:	Mr Franks is a long time talking to Queenie.
Sally:	Here she comes now.
Madge and Sally:	Well, what did he say?
Queenie:	He wants me to play the part.
Sally:	Your wish has come true. You're going to be Dick Whittington?
Queenie:	No, Pearl has arrived. I'm going to be the cat!

Artwork by Paul Davies
Cover design by David Armitage

 First impression 1990
0 00 313545 4

Published by Collins Educational
London and Glasgow
Typeset by Kalligraphic Design Ltd, Horley
Printed and Bound by Bell and Bain Ltd., Glasgow